Presented to:

_____

From:

_____

Date:

_____

All Scripture quotations are taken from the King James Version of the Bible.
07 06 05 04 03 10 9 8 7 6 5 4 3 2 1

Have Yourself a Merry Little Christmas
ISBN 1-56292-935-6
Copyright © 2003 by Bordon Books
6532 E. 71 Street, Suite 105
Tulsa, OK 74133

Published by Honor Books
An Imprint of Cook Communications Ministries
4050 Lee Vance View
Colorado Springs, Colorado 89018

Developed by Bordon Books

"Have Yourself A Merry Little Christmas," by Hugh Martin and Ralph Blane
©1943 (Renewed) Metro-Goldwyn-Mayer Inc. ©1944 (Renewed) EMI Feist Catalog Inc.
All Rights Reserved Warner Bros. Publications U.S. Inc., Miami, FL. 33014

Have Yourself a
Merry Little
Christmas

HB

Have Yourself a Merry Little Christmas

Have yourself a merry little Christmas.
Let your heart be light.
From now on our troubles
Will be out of sight.

Have yourself a merry little Christmas.
Make the Yule-tide gay,
From now on our troubles
Will be miles away.

Here we are as in olden days,
Happy golden days of yore,
Faithful friends who are dear to us
Gather near to us once more.

Through the years we all will be together
If the Fates allow,
Hang a shining star
On the highest bough,
And have yourself
A merry little Christmas now.

About the Music

"Have Yourself a Merry Little Christmas" was introduced in the film *Meet Me in St. Louis* by Judy Garland in 1944. Garland also recorded the song for Decca Records in 1944.

Introduction

The customs and traditions surrounding Christmas have changed significantly through the years. Trees, which were originally elaborately situated on tables, were replaced by full-sized trees perched in living rooms. Candles gave way to electric lights, and handmade gifts were replaced by store-bought fare. One thing has not changed, however. The Holy Infant born in a manger in Bethlehem is still the central figure of our celebrations.

We pray that as you move through these pages, you will catch a glimpse of the many aspects of this beloved time of peace and joy, that you will revel in the customs, the music, the poetry. And we also pray that you will understand as never before the significance of God's precious gift to you and to all mankind.

Christmas is the season
for kindling the fire of hospitality
in the hall,
the genial flame of charity
in the heart.

For centuries men have kept an appointment with Christmas. Christmas means fellowship, feasting, giving and receiving, a time of good cheer, home.

Take Christ out of Christmas,
and December becomes
the bleakest and most
colorless month of the year.

What Makes Christmas?

"What makes Christmas?"
I asked my soul,
And this answer came back to me:
"It is the Glory of heaven come down
In the hearts of humanity—
Come in the spirit and heart of a Child,
And it matters not what we share
At Christmas; it is not Christmas at all
Unless the Christ Child be there."

Gift Giving

Gift giving was first practiced by the Romans, who customarily exchanged small gifts during the winter months. The Christmas gift giving we know probably began when early Christians, inspired by the belief that the shepherds and Magi took gifts to the Christ Child, began to observe the custom.

for the Record

In the 1870s, retailers latched on to the idea of marketing store-bought gifts. Toy soldiers, expensive porcelain dolls, and elaborate train sets were heavily advertised in newspapers, catalogs, and shop windows.

Did You Know?

In the early tradition of Christmas, people made and exchanged handmade gifts. This custom has all but been forgotten, however, since the affluent 1950s. Many feel it might be time to reinstate this more personal approach. Benefits include: less stress, less expense, less waste, and more time to reflect on the true meaning of the Christmas season.

Making a Rose Sachet

To make a Rose Sachet you will need a 12 x 8-inch piece of fabric and a 12 to 18 inch length of ribbon.

To fill three sachets, you will need:

4 oz rose petals

1 oz whole rosebuds

$^1/2$ oz whole cloves

12 oz orrisroot powder

2 drops damask rose oil

Christmas Tip

Suggestions for handmade gifts include: baked goods, original poems, stories, and paintings, help with yard work and other chores, and of course, the one Christmas gift every child who attended elementary school in the '50s made for his or her mother—the always useful handwoven potholder!

Christmas Tip

Suggestions for ecologically sensitive
gifts: low-flow shower heads,
rechargeable flashlights, fire
extinguishers, tickets to a play,
and BOOKS!

The Whole Year Through

Remember while December
Brings the only Christmas day.
In the year let there be Christmas
In the things you do and say;
Wouldn't life be worth the living
Wouldn't dreams be coming true
If we kept the Christmas spirit
All the whole year through?

Many merry Christmases, friendships, great accumulation of cheerful recollections, affection on earth, and Heaven at last for all of us.

Did You Know?

Turkey rules the Christmas feast only in England, France, Spain, and the United States. Goose is the fowl of choice in Austria, Denmark, and the Alsace region of France.

In the United States, ham and pheasant have earned a significant spot as the centerpiece of the Christmas Day feast.

The Turkey and the Ant

How bless'd, how envied, were our life,
Could we but 'scape the poulterer's knife!
But man, curs'd man, on Turkeys preys,
And Christmas shortens all our days:
Sometimes with oysters we combine,
Sometimes assist the savory chine;
From the low peasant to the lord,
The Turkey smokes on every board.

Deck the Halls

Deck the hall with boughs of holly,
Fa la la la la, la la la la.
'Tis the season to be jolly,
Fa la la la la, la la la la.
Don we now our gay apparel,
Fa la la, la la la, la la la.
Troll the ancient Yuletide carol.
Fa la la la la, la la la la.

See the blazing Yule before us,
Fa la la la la, la la la la.
Strike the harp and join the chorus,
Fa la la la la, la la la la.
Follow me in merry measure,
Fa la la, la la la, la la la.
While I tell the Yuletide treasure,
Fa la la la la, la la la la.

About the Music

"Deck the Halls" is based on an old Welsh tune,
popular in the 1700s. Mozart was known to enjoy
playing the song.

The words were added in America
sometime after 1800.

Did You Know?

The halls were traditionally decked with ivy, yew, holly, fir cones, and other natural materials. The custom of decorating with evergreens at Christmas was first a Roman custom, signifying eternal life. Holly has its own special meaning as well. The holly's spiked leaves are said to represent Christ's crown of thorns, and the bright, red berries His blood.

Did You Know?

In 1942-43, the War Production Board asked the nation's cities to refrain from using outdoor Christmas lighting. Even in 1946, postwar America suffered a shortage of wiring and other materials, thus dimming out-of-doors displays.

Did You Know?

In 1947, 100 downtown street poles in Omaha, Nebraska, were decorated with garlands, balsam fir wreaths, and lights. By 1949, a Yule-lighting drive raised $14,500. On Thanksgiving Day, 40,000 people gathered to welcome the Christmas season. The lights were on in Omaha and across America once again.

Homemade Clay for Tree Ornaments

1 cup cornstarch
2 cups baking soda
1 $1/2$ cups cold water
String
Paint
Clear shellac

Instructions: In saucepan, stir thoroughly cornstarch, baking soda, and water. Heat, stirring constantly until mixture reaches a slightly moist, mashed-potato consistency. Pour onto a plate and cover with a damp cloth. When cooled, knead like dough. Roll out to a quarter-inch thickness and cut with a knife or cookie cutter. Pierce a hole near the top for the string. Let dry; paint. When paint is dry, finish with a coat of shellac.

Christmas Games

A popular Christmas party trick in the late 1800s was "eating a candle." Understandably, this trick was most effective in the evening. Tricksters would cut an apple as round and long as their thumbs. Then an almond was stuck into the top to serve as a wick. When lit, the almond burned for a full minute, convincing the guests that it was indeed a candle. Then the wick was removed and the "candle" was eaten to the oohs and aahs of the crowd.

Here's to the day of good will,
cold weather, and warm hearts!

*Let's dance and sing
and make good cheer,
for Christmas comes
but once a year.*

Be merry all, be merry all,
With holly dress and festive hall;
Prepare the song, the feast, the ball,
To welcome merry Christmas.

Did You Know?

In 1942, patriotic Americans made ornaments rather than purchasing them. Magazines provided patterns and directions for making these handmade decorations from non-priority war items.

Did You Know?

In the 1950s, big department stores in cities like New York, Chicago, and Philadelphia began the custom of constructing elaborate window displays during the Christmas season. These were aimed at enticing shoppers inside for Christmas shopping.

So now is come our joyful'st feast
Let every man be jolly;
Each room with ivy leaves is drest
And every post with holly.
And while thus inspired we sing,
Let all the streets with echoes ring
Woods and hills and everything
Bear witness we are merry.

The Christmas Tree

A popular legend holds that Martin Luther cut down the first Christmas tree and placed candles on it to represent the starry skies of Bethlehem on the night of Christ's birth. Under it, he placed a nativity scene, which included Mary, Joseph, the baby Jesus, and a few animals.

For the Record

An average American household in the 1940s spent about $10 decorating their first Christmas tree and about $3 every year after that to replace broken ornaments. In 1941, a 5-foot-tall Christmas tree could be purchased for about 75 cents.

Did You Know?

In 1951, President Truman said a prayer for peace before lighting the National Christmas Tree. It soon became a Pageant of Peace when a life-sized nativity scene was added to the ceremony, along with eight reindeer from Alaska.

The message of Christmas is that
the visible material world is bound to
the invisible spiritual world.

Did You Know?

President Franklin Pierce was the first to decorate a
Christmas tree at the White House.

A ninety-foot Norway spruce was placed in
Rockefeller Center in 1948.

One of the largest Christmas trees ever seen—
212-feet tall—was erected in Seattle in 1950.

For the Record

The Christmas tree carpet was inspired by the need
to catch wax dripping onto the floor from the
Christmas tree candles. By 1913, it was possible to
purchase beautifully painted carpets. After electric
lights became popular, it had become customary to
place a white sheet under the tree to look like snow.

The Mahogany Tree

Christmas is here;
Winds whistle shrill,
Icy and chill,
Little care we;
Little we fear
Weather without,
Sheltered about
The Mahogany Tree.

For the Record

In the 1940s, a new way of flocking the Christmas tree became popular. It was originally accomplished by throwing water and then flour onto the tree—a messy enterprise. The newer procedure directed the erstwhile decorator to mix a box of Lux soap with two cups of water and brush it onto the tree, then simply let it dry. The result: the tree appeared to be lightly frosted with newly fallen snow.

Christmas Tip

In 1960, *Better Homes and Gardens* magazine suggested the following formula for putting lights on your tree: Take the height of the tree in feet, and multiply it times the width of the tree at its widest part, times three. For example, a 6-foot-tall tree that is 4 feet wide (times three) would need 72 lights.

Christmas Snowballs

2 cups sifted flour
$1/4$ cup sugar
$1/2$ tsp salt
1 cup butter
2 tsp vanilla
2 $1/2$ cups finely chopped nuts

Instructions: Sift flour, sugar, and salt together; work into the butter and vanilla. Add 2 cups of nuts and mix well. Shape into $1/2$-inch balls. Roll half the balls in remaining nuts. Place on greased cookie sheets; bake in a moderate oven at 350 degrees for about 40 minutes. Roll plain cookies in powdered sugar and bake for the same amount of time.

Here We Come A-Caroling

Here we come a-caroling
Among the leaves so green;
Here we come a-wand'ring,
So fair to be seen.

Chorus:
Love and joy come to you
And to you glad Christmas too.
And God bless you and send you
A Happy New Year,
And God send you a Happy New Year.

God bless the master of this house,
Likewise the mistress too,
And all the little children
That round this table go.

Chorus:
Love and joy come to you
And to you glad Christmas too.
And God bless you and send you
A Happy New Year,
And God send you a Happy New Year.

About the Music

The 1871 publication *Christmas Carols Old and New* inspired the revival of many of the old Christmas carols as well as the writing of new ones. The custom of organized caroling—groups going door-to-door singing carols for their neighbors—began in Victorian England before becoming popular in America.

About the Music

Caroling was originally a rowdy and pagan practice. St. Francis of Assisi was among those who introduced sacred music in an effort to Christianize the custom. Pious words were put to standard tunes, and this metamorphosis was targeted primarily at Christmas, emphasizing the sufferings of Christ and the plight of the Christ Child.

Wassail

1 gallon apple cider (apple bits strained out)
1 tsp ground cloves
1 tsp ground allspice
1 tsp ground nutmeg
1 tsp ground cinnamon
1 6-oz can frozen lemonade, thawed
1 6-oz can frozen orange juice, thawed
1/2 cup firmly packed brown sugar

Instructions: Combine 2 cups apple cider and spices in a large Dutch oven; bring to a boil. Reduce heat and simmer 10 minutes. Add remaining cider and other ingredients and heat until very hot. Do not boil.

Makes 4 $^1/_2$ quarts.

Happy Wassailing!

Sing we all merrily
Christmas is here,
The day that we love best
of days in the year.

Bring for the holly,
The box, and the bay.
Deck out our cottage
For glad Christmas Day.

Sing we all merrily,
Draw round the fire,
Sister and brother,
Grandson and sire.

The family, the story, the carol, and the gift. These four when divested of their present secularistic trappings give us the pure Christian element of Christmas. I do believe that quite a case can be made for a thoroughly enjoyable Christmas with every whit as much spirit and color using only these four ingredients.

Christmas in the Heart

It is Christmas in the mansion,
Yule log fires and silken frocks;
It is Christmas in the cottage,
Mother's filling little socks.

It is Christmas on the highway,
In the thronging, busy mart;
But the dearest, truest Christmas
Is the Christmas in the heart.

Edible Holiday Candles for Kids

Ingredients:
2 bananas
4 sugar cookies
4 maraschino cherries
4 slices of canned pineapple
4 teaspoons of whipped cream
Place one sugar cookie on each plate.
Lay a pineapple slice on top of each cookie.
Stand $1/2$ banana in the hole of each pineapple.
Top the banana with a bit of whipped cream and a
cherry.

Christmas Bells

I heard the bells on Christmas Day
Their old, familiar carols play,
And wild and sweet
The words repeat
Of peace on earth, good will to men!

Then pealed the bells more loud and deep:
   "God is not dead, nor doth He sleep;
   The wrong shall fail, the right prevail,
   With peace on earth, good will to men."

About the Music

"I Heard the Bells on Christmas Day" is one of the few poems by Henry Wadsworth Longfellow that has been put to music. The tune was written by an English organist and composer, John Baptiste Calkin. The bass notes were written to sound like the ringing of a bell.

About the Music

Longfellow wrote this beloved poem on Christmas
Day in 1863. The Civil War was at its height, and
the poet was in deep despair. Hearing the Christmas
bells chiming, he realized that God was great
enough to overcome the world's strife.
The poem is his prayer for peace.

Did You Know?

For centuries, bells have been used to announce both sad and happy events. Along the way, they became particularly associated with Christmas celebrations. Now bells announce the season celebrating Christ's birth from atop churches, in shopping districts, and in our homes.

Did You Know?

In the days of Olde England, groups of traveling singers entertained for food or pay. Referred to as waits, these groups were popular at Christmastime. "We Wish You a Merry Christmas" is one of the songs commonly performed by the waits.

We Wish You a Merry Christmas

We wish you a Merry Christmas
We wish you a Merry Christmas
We wish you a Merry Christmas
And a Happy New Year!

Good tidings we bring
For you and your kin.
Good tidings for Christmas
And a Happy New Year!

When Christmas-tide comes
in like a bride,
With holly and ivy clad,
Twelve days in the year,
much mirth and good cheer
In every household is had.

*H*eap on the wood!
—the wind is chill;
But let it whistle as it will,
We'll keep our Christmas merry still.

Now Christmas is come
Let's beat up the drum,
And call all our neighbors together;
And when they appear,
Let's make them such cheer
As will keep out the wind and the weather.

May each be found thus as the year
circles round,
With mirth and good humor each
Christmas be crowned,
And may all who have plenty of riches in store
With their bountiful blessings make
happy the poor;
For never as yet it was counted a crime,
To be merry and cheery at that happy time.

Jingle Bells

Dashing through the snow
In a one-horse open sleigh
Through the fields we go
Laughing all the way.
Bells on bob-tail ring
Making spirits bright
What fun it is to ride and sing
A sleighing song tonight.

Chorus:

Jingle bells, jingle bells
Jingle all the way,
Oh what fun it is to ride
In a one-horse open sleigh.
Oh jingle bells, jingle bells
Jingle all the way,
Oh what fun it is to ride
In a one-horse open sleigh.

About the Music

"Jingle Bells" was written by James Pierpont around the middle of the 19th century. It was originally entitled "One-Horse Open Sleigh."

Pierpont told a neighbor, "I have a little tune in my head," and he asked to use her piano to try it out. Mrs. Waterman, Pierpont's neighbor, later wrote in her diary that she had helped him compose the chorus of this Christmas favorite.

Christmas is but a big love affair to remove the wrinkles of the year with kindly remembrances.

Instead of being a time of unusual behavior,
Christmas is perhaps the only time in the year
when people can obey their natural impulses
and express their true sentiments without feeling
self-conscious and perhaps, foolish.

O you merry, merry Souls,
Christmas is a coming,
We shall have flowing bowls,
Dancing, piping, drumming.

The cock sat up in the yew tree,
The hen came chuckling by,
I wish you a merry Christmas
And a good fat pig in the sty.

At Christmas play and
make good cheer,
For Christmas comes just
once a year.

God Rest Ye Merry Gentlemen

God rest ye merry gentlemen,
Let nothing ye dismay,
Remember Christ our Savior
Was born on Christmas day,
To save us all from Satan's power
When we were gone astray;

O tidings of comfort and joy,
Comfort and joy,
O tidings of comfort and joy.

Now to the Lord sing praises,
All ye within this place.
And with true love and brotherhood
Each other now embrace; this holy tide of
Christmas
All others doth deface:

O tidings of comfort and joy,
Comfort and joy,
O tidings of comfort and joy.

About the Music

In his Christmas favorite, *A Christmas Carol*, Charles
Dickens has included a young boy singing this
wonderful old carol, "God Rest Ye Merry Gentlemen."
Dickens' story is credited with reviving the widespread
celebration of Christmas.

About the Music

The durability of this old carol, "God Rest Ye Merry Gentlemen," is said to be the result of the way the first verse expresses the essence of the Christmas story in the words of the common man.

The way to Christmas lies through
an ancient gate. . . . It is a little gate,
child-high, child-wide, and there is a password:
"Peace on earth to men of good will."
May you, this Christmas, become as a little child
again and enter into His kingdom.

Glory to God in the highest,
and on earth peace,
good will toward men!

The Christmas Box

The tradition of giving to charity during the Christmas season was practiced even before the custom of exchanging gifts with family and friends. The Christmas Box was placed in the church on Christmas Day. Worshippers placed their contributions in the box before or after the Christmas service. The next day, commonly known as "Boxing Day," the money was gathered and distributed to the poor.

At Christmas-tide the open hand
Scatters its bounty o'er sea and land,
And none are left to grieve alone,
For love is heaven and claims its own.

It is Christmas every time you let God love others through you . . . . Yes, it is Christmas every time you smile at your brother and offer him your hand.

Christmas Candles

Some believe the custom of lighting candles at
Christmas is associated with the Jewish Hanukkah
or Feast of Lights. Others identify the candle with
Christ, the light of the world. Candles were
originally placed not only on or near the
Christmas tree but also in windows and various
places throughout the home.

Did You Know?

The Portuguese have a tradition of
placing candles in every window of
their homes at Christmas. This signifies that all
persons are welcome to visit—friends, and
especially strangers.

Did You Know?

In Scandinavian countries, it is the custom to
burn candles in their homes during the
Christmas season and throughout the
long winter months. They believe that the soft
glow lights up their homes and their hearts.

For the Record

In the 1930s, Christmas tree safety became a big issue. Americans were urged to discontinue the use of Christmas candles on trees and in windows in favor of electric lights.

For the Record

Aluminum Christmas trees became the rage in the mid-1950s. These sprang from the popularity of the foil decorations used in the 1940s. For these trees, electric lights were not an option. Floodlights or revolving color wheels were used to light the trees.

Christmas Cards

The Christmas card is a relatively new idea, dating back to the 1840s. The first commercially made cards looked a great deal like valentines, probably because they were put out by firms already selling Valentine cards.

Did You Know?

Mr. Henry Cole was most probably the first person to send out a Christmas card. It consisted of a sentiment expressed below the picture of a family, which was brimming with good cheer. One thousand of the hand-colored cards were put on sale in 1946.

For the Record

More than two billion holiday cards
are sold each year in the United States—
enough to fill a football field
10 stories high!

He comes, the brave old Christmas.

His sturdy steps I hear;

We will give him a hearty welcome,

For he comes but once a year!

Music, merry and clear;
Eve, the crown of the year;
Romping of bright girls and boys;
Reindeer that bring them the toys;
Yule-log softly aglow.

Cold of the sky and the snow;
Hearth where they hang up the hose;
Reel which the old folks propose;
Icicles seen through the pane;
Sleigh-bells, with tinkling refrain;
Tree with gifts all a-bloom
Mistletoe hung in the room;
Anthems we all love to hear;
St. Nicholas—joy of the year!

Did You Know?

The U.S. Post Office produced its
first Christmas stamp in 1962.

Did You Know?

Christmas seals were the thoughtful idea of a postal clerk from Denmark named Einar Holboell. While sorting Christmas mail in 1903, Holboell remembered those children suffering with tuberculosis. He pitched the idea to sell a penny stamp to be placed on mail in addition to regular postage. The proceeds were to help build a hospital for the children of Copenhagen.

Joy to the World

Joy to the world, the Lord is come
Let earth receive her King.
Let every heart prepare him room,
And heaven and nature sing,
And heaven and nature sing,
And heaven and heaven and nature sing.

Joy to the world the Savior reigns
Let men their songs employ,
While fields and floods
Rocks, hills and plains
Repeat the sounding joy
Repeat the sounding joy
Repeat, repeat the sounding joy.

About the Music

"Joy to the World," one of the most joyous hymns of the Christmas season, was written by poet Isaac Watts, who penned some of the most beautiful hymns in the English language. The poet also wrote the cradle song, "Hush, My Dear, Lie Still" and "Slumber, Holy Angels Guard Thy Bed," which became a children's Christmas favorite.

About the Music

At the age of 18, young Isaac Watts complained to his father about the tacky and graceless songs being sung in the church. His father answered, "If you don't like the hymns, write better ones!" Isaac did just that! He presented a new hymn to his home congregation each Sunday morning for two hundred and twenty-two consecutive Sundays.

For the Record

In 1954, George Balanchine recreated Tchaikovsky's ballet, the Nutcracker, and made it a gift to the people of New York City. It was an immediate hit and is now produced by ballet troupes around the country.

The Christmas Story

[Mary] brought forth her firstborn son, and
wrapped him in swaddling clothes, and laid him
in a manger; because there was no room
for them in the inn.

LUKE 2:7 KJV

When mother-love makes all things bright,
When joy comes with the morning light,
When children gather round their tree,
Thou Christmas Babe, we sing of thee!

A Christmas Carol

There's a song in the air!
There's a star in the sky!
There's a mother's deep prayer
And a Baby's low cry!
And the star rains its fire
while the Beautiful sing,
For the manger of Bethlehem
cradles a King.

Once in royal David's city
Stood a lowly cattle shed,
Where a Mother laid her Baby
In a manger for His bed:
Mary was that Mother mild,
Jesus Christ her little Child.

There were in the same country shepherds abiding in the field, keeping watch over their flock by night. And, lo, the angel of the Lord came upon them, and the glory of the Lord shone round about them: and they were sore afraid. And the angel said unto them, Fear not: for, behold, I bring you good tidings of great joy, which shall be to all people.

LUKE 2:8-10 KJV

The simple shepherds heard
the voice of an angel and
found their Lamb;
the wise men saw
the light of a star and
found their Wisdom.

In the Bleak Midwinter

What can I give him
Poor as I am?
If I were a shepherd,
I would bring a lamb;
If I were a wise man,
I would do my part;
Yet what I can give him—
Give my heart.

Bethlehem's Babe

O little, feeble, smiling Babe,
To Thee I bow the knee;
I worship where Thou hast been laid
And fondly bend o'er Thee;
At other times, I'll praise Thy might—
But Thou art just my Babe tonight!

When Jesus was born in Bethlehem of Judaea in the days of Herod the king, behold, there came wise men from the east to Jerusalem, saying, Where is he that is born King of the Jews? For we have seen his star in the east, and are come to worship him. When Herod the king had heard these things, he was troubled, and all Jerusalem with him.

MATTHEW 2:1-3 KJV

When they were come into the house, they saw the young child with Mary his mother, and fell down, and worshipped him: and when they had opened their treasures, they presented unto him gifts; gold, and frankincense, and myrrh. And being warned of God in a dream that they should not return to Herod, they departed into their own country another way.

MATTHEW 2:11-12 KJV

The Gifts of the Magi

The Bible says that the Magi took gifts to the Christ Child—gifts that acknowledged his deity, purity, and the role He would play in the redemption of mankind.

The gifts of the Magi were:

Gold: The Child was presented with gold as a symbol of his Kingship and a reminder that we owe God our virtue.

Frankincense: At the time of Christ's birth, frankincense was an expensive form of incense and it represents Christ as God. It reminds us that we owe God our prayers.

Myrrh: This ointment is thought to have medicinal qualities. It is a symbol of Christ as healer and reminds us that we owe God our suffering.

117

We Three Kings

They laid their offerings at his feet;
The gold was their tribute to a King,
The frankincense, with its odor sweet,
Was for the Priest, the Paraclete,
The myrrh for the body's burying.

The Holy Star

Yet doth the Star of Bethlehem shed
A luster pure and sweet,
And still it leads, as once it led,
To the Messiah's feet.

O Father, may that holy star
Grow every year more bright,
And send its glorious beams afar
To fill the world with light.

To travel the road to Bethlehem
is to keep a rendezvous with wonder,
to answer the call of wisdom,
and to bow the knee in worship.

for the Record

Tradition says that there were three wise men who followed the brilliant star to Bethlehem's stable. But the Bible doesn't actually mention how many wise men came from the East to worship the Christ Child. It says only that three gifts were given: gold, frankincense, and myrrh.

The Nativity Scene

Saint Francis of Assisi is credited with the idea of creating a model of the nativity. He made ready a manger or crib and added hay, an ox, and a donkey. Once he had recreated the scene, it is said that he stood before the manger, bathed in tears and overflowing with joy.

Did You Know?

Carved miniature models of the Nativity soon became popular. The clothing worn by the wise men changed with the styles adopted by kings of the day, but the shepherds changed very little in regard to dress. In the seventeenth century, the angels were given powdered wigs and hats trimmed with feathers.

Away in a Manger

Away in a manger, no crib for a bed,
The little Lord Jesus laid down His sweet head.
The stars in the sky looked down where He lay,
The little Lord Jesus, asleep on the hay.

The cattle are lowing, the Baby awakes,
But little Lord Jesus, no crying He makes;
I love Thee, Lord Jesus, look down from the sky
And stay by my cradle til morning is nigh.

About the Music

It isn't known conclusively who penned the words to "Away in a Manger." Many believe it was Martin Luther, probably because James Murray, who composed the music, called it "Luther's Cradle Hymn."

Did You Know?

The Madonna della Grazie, built by Capuchin monks, is one of the most unique and costly nativity scenes in Italy. A grotto of Sardinian cork rises to a height of eighteen feet. The three kings are elaborately carved figures. The shepherds move down a mountainside to the manger, where Mary and Joseph are watching over the Christ Child.

Selfishness makes
Christmas a burden;
love makes it a delight.

The Christ-child stood
at Mary's knee
His hair was like a crown,
And all the flowers looked up at Him,
And all the stars
looked down.

Christmas is the gift from heaven
Of God's Son given for free;
If Christmas isn't found in your heart,
You won't find it under the tree.

O Come, All Ye Faithful

O come, all ye faithful,
Joyful and triumphant.
O come ye, O come ye to Bethlehem;
Come and behold him,
Born the King of angels;

Chorus:

O come, let us adore him,
O come, let us adore him,
O come, let us adore him,
Christ the Lord.

About the Music

There are more than forty translations of the Christmas hymn, "O Come, All Ye Faithful." The version we have come to know and love is the work of Frederick Oakeley, a Catholic priest. It first appeared in Murray's Hymnal in 1852.

About the Music

The earliest words and melody of *O Come, All Ye Faithful* were found in a collection of hymns compiled in England about 1750 by John Francis Wade. Some believe Wade wrote the hymn, while others think it was a much older carol sung while dancing 'round the manger.

Did You Know?

The most popular Christmas gift in 1957
was the hula hoop!
Everybody was asking for one.

For the Record

The traditional English Christmas dessert, plum pudding, contains lots of dried fruit but nary a plum!

Sugarplums aren't plums either. They are generally thought to be round or oval chocolates filled with nougats or creams. In other words, Valentine candy!

Christmas Figgy Pudding

$^1\!/2$ pound dried figs
$^1\!/4$ cup fluffy bread crumbs
1 cup almonds or walnuts, chopped
1 cup light brown sugar
$^3\!/4$ cup candied citrus peel
3 tbsp. melted butter
4 eggs, beaten
$^1\!/2$ tsp. cinnamon
$^1\!/4$ tsp. nutmeg

Hard Sauce
1 cup butter
1 cup powdered sugar
1 tbsp. vanilla

Instructions: Chop the figs and mix with crumbs. Brown the almonds or walnuts. Mix with other ingredients. Put the mixture into a greased mold and bake at 325 degrees for 1 hour.

Hard Sauce: Beat 1 cup of butter for about 2 minutes. Add a cup of icing sugar and 1 tbsp vanilla. Beat for 5 minutes. Pour over hot pudding.

Merry Christmas in Other Languages

Denmark: Glaedelig Jul
England: Merry Christmas
France: Joyeux Noël
Germany: Fröhliche Weinachten
Greece: Kala Christougena
Holland: Zalig Kerstfeest

Italy: Buon Natale
Japan: Meri Kurisumasu
Mexico: Feliz Navidad
Norway: Gledelig Jul
Poland: Wesolych Swiat
Portugal: Boas Festas
Romania: Sarbatori Vesele
Spain: Felices Pascuas
Sweden: Glad Jul
Wales: Nadolog Llawen

Good Saint Nick

The real St. Nicholas, who was the inspiration for Santa Claus, was an early Christian bishop. He lived in the fourth century and was known for his remarkable generosity. Possessed of an unusual sympathy for the many poor, he often went out in disguise and distributed presents, especially to children.

$\mathcal{L}$egend has it that St. Nicholas took pity on the three daughters of a nobleman who had lost his fortune. The young women had no money for dowries. When the eldest reached marriageable age, Nicholas went to their home one night and threw a bag of gold through the window. The act was repeated when the second and third daughters came of age.

After the girl's father discovered that St. Nicholas had been his daughter's benefactor, he spread the word far and near. Soon he was given credit for most unexpected, anonymous gifts.

A related legend says that the custom of the Christmas stocking was inspired when St. Nicholas tossed a bag of gold into the window for one of the young women and it fell into a stocking hung near the chimney to dry.

Did You Know?

Thomas Nast is the person who had the most to do with the American image of Santa Claus. Between 1863 and 1886, Nast produced a series of Christmas drawings, depicting Santa with twinkling eyes, rosy cheeks, and a plump belly. In each drawing, Santa was seen going about his work making toys, filling stockings, checking on the behavior of some unsuspecting youngster, decorating Christmas trees, flying in his sleigh, and many other things.

For the Record

The painting by Haddon Sundblom of Santa Claus drinking a Coca Cola is the source of yet another Santa image. Sundblom's full-color advertisements, produced during the 1930s, introduced Santa in a red suit rather than a fur coat.

Did You Know?

The custom of leaving milk and cookies by the
tree
for Santa Claus became popular in the 1940s.
Debates ensued concerning which cookies
Santa preferred. No wonder Santa sported
such a weighty girth!

Up on the housetop reindeer pause,
Out jumps good old Santa Claus;
Down through the chimney with lots of toys
All for the little ones, Christmas joys.

Did You Know?

The story Rudolph the Red-Nosed Reindeer
was originally conceived by Robert L. May for the
advertising department of Montgomery Ward
and used as a give-away item for the
Christmas season of 1939.

For the Record

In 1949, Gene Autry and Bing Crosby recorded Rudolph's story, which had been put to music by Johnny Marks, who was also the author of "Holly Jolly Christmas."

It is good to be children sometimes,
and never better than at Christmas,
when its mighty Founder was a child himself.

May each be found thus as the year circles round,
With mirth and good humor each Christmas be crowned,
And may all who have plenty of riches in store
With their bountiful blessings make happy the poor;
For never as yet it was counted a crime,
To be merry and cheery at that happy time.

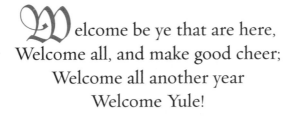

Welcome be ye that are here,
Welcome all, and make good cheer;
Welcome all another year
Welcome Yule!

Welcome be Thou, heavenly King,
Welcome born on this morning,
Welcome, for whom we shall sing
Welcome Yule!

Man, be merry
As birds on berry,
And all thy care let away.

May God bless your Christmas;
May it last until Easter.

The twelfth day of Christmas,
My true love sent to me
Twelve lords a-leaping,
Eleven ladies dancing,
Ten pipers piping,
Nine drummers drumming,
Eight maids a-milking,

Seven swans a-swimming,
Six geese a-laying,
Five gold rings,
Four calling birds,
Three French hens,
Two turtle doves, and
A partridge in a pear tree.

The Holly and the Ivy

The holly and the ivy,
When they are both full grown,
Of all the trees that are in the wood,
The holly bears the crown,
The rising of the sun
And the running of the deer,
The playing of the merry organ,
Sweet singing in the choir.

The Christmas message is that there is
hope for a ruined humanity—
hope of pardon, hope of peace with God,
hope of glory—because at the Father's will
Jesus Christ became poor and was
born in a stable so that thirty years later
He might hang on a cross.

Morning Star, O cheering sight!
Ere thou cam'st, how dark the night!
Jesus mine, in me shine,
Fill my heart with light divine.

Acknowledgments

Washington Irving (8, 68), W. J. Ronald Tucker (9), A. F. Wells (10), Charles Dickens (19, 150), Author Unknown (11, 18, 31, 40, 54, 56, 129, 153a, 156), John Gay (21), Sir George Alexander Macfarren (32), W.R. Spencer (33), George Wither (36), William M. Thackeray (43), John D. Tate (55), Henry Wadsworth Longfellow (58, 118), English Traditional (66), Sir Walter Scott (67), 18th century broadside (69, 151), John Wanamaker (73), Frances C. Farley (74), Christmas Entertainments 1740 (75), W. S. W. Anson, ed (76), Thomas Tusser (77), Angelo Patri (82), Margaret E. Sangster (85), Mother Teresa (86), English, 19th century (95), From St. Nicholas, January 1897 (97), Tudor Jenks (107), Josiah Gilbert Holland (108) A.F. Alexander (109), Fulton John Sheen (111), Christina Rossetti (112), Henry W. Frost (113), William Cullen Bryant (119), John Knight (120), G. K. Chesterton (127), Charlotte Carpenter (128), Benjamin Handby (147), English, 15th century (152), Scandinavian Blessing (153b), Nursery Rhyme (155), J.I. Packer (157), Moravian hymn (158).

If you have enjoyed this book, or if it has impacted
your life, we would like to hear from you.

Please contact us at:

Honor Books
An imprint of Cook Communications Ministries
4050 Lee Vance View
Colorado Springs, CO 89018

Or by e-mail at cookministries.com